To Marcus, Ewan and Elspeth – all of whom were born in Chatham.

A CENTURY of
CHATHAM

Fire at the former Ritz cinema, September 1998. Following this event, the building, which had become a bingo hall, was entirely replaced. (*Medway Today*)

A CENTURY of
CHATHAM

PHILIP MacDOUGALL

The
History
Press

First published in the United Kingdom in 2002 by Sutton Publishing Limited

This new paperback edition first published in 2010 by The History Press
The History Press
The Mill, Brimscombe Port,
Stroud, Gloucestershire, GL5 2QG
www.thehistorypress.co.uk

British Library Cataloguing in Publication Data
A catalogue record for this book is available from the British Library.

ISBN 978-0-7509-5801-4

Illustrations

Front endpaper: Military Road, *c.* 1905. A tram bound for Chatham cemetery passes a range of shops that are now buried under Mountbatten House. This road was once the real centre of Chatham, with all trams terminating at the Town Hall. (Author)
Back endpaper: The Festival of Cultures, 5 September 1988. (Author)
Half title page: Chatham railway station, 1 September 1939. With war imminent, the children of St Michael's School are about to travel into the Kentish countryside. The dockyard was expected to be a major target for aerial bombardment. (*Medway Today*)
Title page: The Tall Ships Race, July 1985. In the basin of the former dockyard a number of the tall ships assembled for this race were thrown open to the visiting public. It was one of the earliest public events to be held in this area of the yard following its closure some sixteen months earlier. (Author)

Typesetting and origination by Sutton Publishing Limited
Printed and bound in England

Contents

Festival of Culture, September 1988. Chatham has long been a multi-cultural community, the army, navy and dockyard attracting recruits from throughout the world. To celebrate this cultural diversity, the North Kent Festival of Culture was held that year in Victoria Gardens. (Author)

Introduction

At the beginning of the twentieth century Chatham was a naval town. By the end of that same century it had entirely lost this connection. One by one, the various facilities built to service the navy were closed and lost to the town. For the most part, this took place after the Second World War, so that Chatham was predominantly a naval town until the 1950s. An early casualty, however, was the Melville Royal Navy Hospital, which once stood opposite the dockyard main gate. Its closure was not the result of any naval cutbacks, but was due to the construction of a much larger hospital in Gillingham. Upon closure, the Melville Hospital site was presented to the Royal Marines, the buildings eventually being used as their pay and records office. When the Marines departed from Chatham, the area was given over to municipal housing, leading to the construction of the present-day Melville Court.

The first of those postwar losses was that of the Royal Marines themselves. Their extensive barracks which once lined Dock Road were abandoned in 1950 and demolished in 1960. The site now houses purpose-built offices that were originally constructed for the Lloyds insurance company. A further loss at this time was the Ordnance Wharf situated along the river frontage immediately to the south of the dockyard. First established during the seventeenth century, it had been responsible for repair and maintenance of ships' ordnance. The most severe losses came in the 1980s, with the closure of both the dockyard and the naval barracks; this was announced by Defence Secretary John Nott in June 1981, with closure coming about in 1984. It must be stated at this point that while HMS *Pembroke*, the Chatham naval barracks, together with much of the dockyard's Victorian extension, may be claimed as part of Gillingham, both by name and by common association, they are truly part of Chatham and have therefore been included within the pages of this book.

The navy, throughout most of the twentieth century, has brought considerable wealth and prosperity to the town. In 1901 more than 15,000 families gained an income from employment directly connected to the navy or its civilian facilities. The dockyard alone employed a workforce of about 10,000, while the Royal Navy and Royal Marine Barracks, together with the gun wharf, were all heavily dependent on local civilian labour. In addition, Chatham army barracks, also situated in Dock Road, similarly employed civilian labour. These barracks too had a long history, having been constructed in the eighteenth century to provide accommodation for the troops needed to defend the dockyard in the event of enemy attack.

However, the twentieth century saw decline as well as prosperity. The interwar period in particular was characterized by reduced defence expenditure, resulting in large-scale local unemployment. The situation was only improved by the spectre of Nazi Germany and the subsequent war.

Members of the gun-crew team in training for the Royal Tournament, Chatham Royal Naval Barracks, c. 1950. Closure of the barracks in 1984 brought to an end the town's 400-year-long connection with the Royal Navy. (Imperial War Museum, A34298)

Dependence on the military was not entirely restricted to those directly employed. Many others benefited indirectly. Numerous High Street shops catered for those serving in the barracks as well as those employed in the dockyard. Some of the most important shops were Gieves (army and navy outfitters at 13 Military Road), A. Fleming & Co. (contractor for uniforms to the Admiralty at 60 Military Road) and H. Hales & Son (Admiralty contractor for fruit and vegetables at 259 High Street and 153 New Road). The music halls and theatres of Chatham also benefited from the presence of the army and navy. In particular, Barnard's Palace of Varieties (107 High Street) advertised a 'twice nightly' performance, the earlier 6.20 performance designed for those soldiers and sailors who had to be back in barracks by 8 p.m.

A less savoury part of the town was also a by-product of its military connection. This was the town's red light area, centred around The Brook. In this, and other nearby roads, were the numerous public houses that accommodated many of the town's prostitutes. To counter this, and help protect young recruits from falling into immoral ways, The Brook became the centre of a crusade, with a Royal Navy mission providing classes, meetings and entertainment of a religious, social and educational character. In addition, there were also various rest homes for those in the army and navy. These were designed as an alternative to pubs and brothels, offering a pub atmosphere minus the alcohol. Both the Methodist Church and the Salvation Army ran such houses, and they provided sleeping accommodation, billiards, games, reading rooms and canteens.

The Brook area also contained many small houses, and for the people living there it must have been an unhappy experience, having to walk past the noisy pubs and questionable scenes. Many of these roads – such as George Street, Fair Row and Solomon's Terrace – are now just a memory, buried since the early 1970s under Mountbatten House and the Pentagon shopping centre. Former residents, nostalgic for their old homes, still take delight in locating the exact site of where they once stood, be it under the present-day W.H. Smith's or beneath one of the enclosed courtyards of the Pentagon. Close to these same houses were such additional delights as two slaughterhouses where cows and pigs were killed. Local residents might benefit from receipt of 'chitterlings' (pig intestines) which were considered a great delicacy, while entertainment resulted from the occasional escaping cow. As with Chatham's former red light area and the myriad small houses and numerous pubs, The Brook and Garden Row slaughterhouses have also disappeared.

Another important series of changes witnessed by the town during the twentieth century concerned public and private transport. At the beginning of the century the town was undergoing a definite revolution, with construction of a tramway system that was opened on 17 June 1902. This required a number of road widening schemes that included the complete removal of the old defensive brick arch and gateway that stood across Railway Street. Originally built during the eighteenth century, it also served as a viaduct, with New Road running across the top. The need for its removal was less a matter of age and more a result of its narrowness, the entrance gateway preventing trams

The final Chatham Navy Days, 24 May 1981. One of the stars of the show on that occasion was the ice patrol ship, HMS *Endurance*. The following year she was at the centre of the Falkland Islands conflict – with the subsequent hostilities resulting in the cancellation of the 1982 Navy Days. (Author)

A general view of Chatham from Fort Pitt Fields, c. 1925. Visible are some of the long-since demolished river-side wharves together with the Ordnance Wharf (below St Mary's Church) and the naval dockyard. (Author)

reaching the Town Hall from the direction of Maidstone Road. Because the archway also carried New Road its replacement needed to be of a wide span, yet capable of carrying considerable amounts of traffic. The solution was the present-day girder bridge, officially opened in October 1902. A further important requirement was the construction of a tram depot and power station. These were both situated in the village of Luton about 200 yards short of the tramway terminus at the Hen and Chickens. In their turn, though, the trams were replaced by the petrol-driven buses of the Chatham and District Traction Company, this coming about on 1 October 1930 when thirty-seven Leyland 'Titan' buses suddenly hit the town. Of course, the buses have remained, although the name of the operating company has undergone various changes as the years passed. Paralleling these changes in public transport has been the more gradual but relentless arrival of the motorcar, which now dominates every aspect of town life. To accommodate the needs of the motorist, the Chatham ring road was instituted in 1987, ensuring that every car journey through central Chatham involved a compulsorily extended circulatory journey, while the Medway Tunnel was opened in June 1996.

Another revolution early in the century was the arrival of the cinema. Chatham's first, the Cinema de Luxe, opened in January 1910. It was little more than a converted shop (78–80 High Street) with cramped wooden benches and a constantly flickering picture. Approximately a year later the town's first purpose-built cinema, the National Electric Theatre, was opened at 205 High Street. In 1913 the impressively large Imperial Picture Palace was opened at the east end of the High Street. Over the years a number of other

Chatham, *c.* 1930. A selection of views on a popular postcard that would have been bought in its hundreds by those people living and working in the dockyard, and perhaps by those visiting the town. (Clive Tester)

The Brook, May 1972. This huge vacant space, now the site of the Pentagon, was once occupied by a mass of terraced housing where hundreds of Chatham families lived. (*Kent Today*)

High Street, 1918. Two shops trading at that time were Chatham
Furnishing Stores and H.C. Lawrence & Son. The latter was still
running from the same premises in the 1990s (see page 50).

cinemas appeared in the town, including the Picture Palace (1917), the Invicta (Fullager's Alley, 1916), the Super Regent (High Street, 1938), the Palace Super Cinema (Chatham Hill, 1936) and the Ritz (High Street, 1937).

Perhaps the most disappointing aspect of modern-day Chatham, apart from the victory of the car, is the failure to preserve. Time after time, unique, unusual or generally interesting buildings have been removed for the purpose of modernization or road widening. In part, this is because Chatham has long been designated the commercial heartland of the Medway Towns, with only medieval and Georgian Rochester thought worthy of historic preservation. Yet the borough's many late Georgian and Victorian buildings do have an intrinsic value and some certainly deserved to be preserved. Perhaps this might be the theme of the new century, given that the theme of the old was destruction of all that stood in the way of progress.

Given that the above was written in 2002 for the original edition, it is interesting to note that Chatham has since undergone a further period of massive change. Particularly welcome, to my mind, was the replacement in 2007 of the ridiculous ring road that extended so many traffic journeys. In turn, this has seen demolition in June 2009 of the flyover (named after Sir John Hawkins, naval administrator and slave trader) that effectively destroyed the economic prosperity once enjoyed by the west end of the High Street. A new bus station, adjacent to the Gun Wharf, was given its go-ahead in early 2010, this also a by-product of the on-going major road and infastructural improvements. The dockyard, albeit on the Gillingham-side, has seen the opening of the Dickens World themed attractions (May 2007), with further residential blocks and inevitable supermarkets also being added. Firmly on the Chatham side of the dockyard, this summer sees the opening of the No. 1 Smithery (through £12.5 million of investment money) as a cultural and learning activity centre. Returning to mid-Chatham, the former Gun Wharf is undergoing regeneration in an attempt to enliven its water frontage and make better use of existing historic buildings. Currently, Chatham is in the process of making a bid for World Heritage status, this based on the town being a former industrial-military complex, with much of the evidence for this very much extant and visitable.

Philip MacDougall
June 2010

Landmarks

The bell tower of St Mary's, the former parish church, May 1976. Although the church building itself has an 800-year history, the bell tower dates only to the late nineteenth century, having been completed in 1898. The church was declared redundant in 1974 and now serves as a heritage centre. (Author)

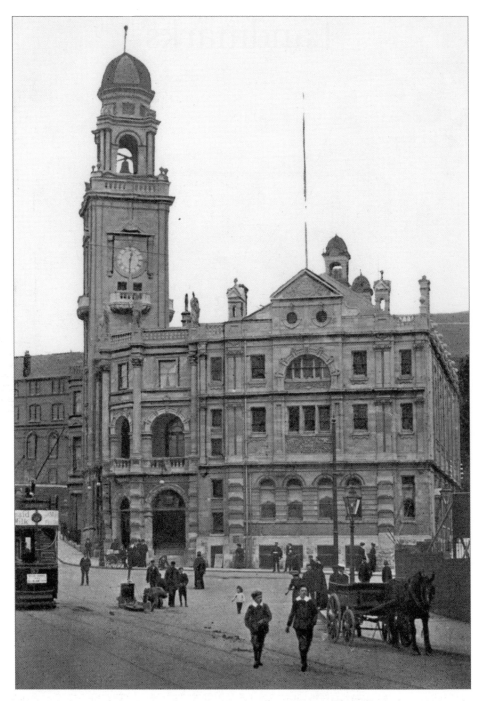

Chatham's showpiece, the Town Hall, *c.* 1908. Chatham was incorporated as a borough in 1890, with elections held in March of the following year. The Town Hall's foundation stone was laid in February 1898, and it was completed two years later. On that occasion, amidst much pomp and ceremony, it was officially opened by former Liberal premier, Lord Rosebery. (Author)

...ham from the River Medway, *c.* 1908. In the centre is the parish church of St Mary's, with the Ordnance Wharf spread ...below. Also visible to the left is the dockyard ropery. The vessel in the foreground is a Thames sailing barge, a type once ...mon around Chatham. These vessels carried every conceivable cargo from building bricks to farm manure. (Author)

...Windmill, Darland
...s, Chatham,
...20. Contrasting
...the hustle and
...e of Chatham
...were the rural
...undings that
...lapped up to the
...of the town. The
...mill at Darland
...s no longer exists,
...ugh the grassy
...s do still provide
...nce to breathe a
...air. (Author)

Boundary Road, c. 1906. Extensive housing was still to be added to this area, and it is probable that the building to the ri
is the drill hall of the Chatham Volunteers. If this is so, then this photo must have been taken shortly after that buildi
completion in 1905. The tower to the left belongs to St John's Church in Railway Street. (Medway Council, Medway Archive
Local Studies Centre)

Entrance to Fort Amherst, c. 1901. A definite clue to the date of this picture is the cupola-topped tower protruding ov
entrenchments on the left. This is the newly completed Town Hall. To the right is Dock Road. The brick wall on the far s
the road belongs to the Ordnance Wharf. St Mary's Church is just out of the picture to the right. (Medway Council, M
Archives & Local Studies Centre)

be Lane, *c*. 1905. This is an unusual view of Chatham, as the photographer has his (or her) back to the Town Hall – which ⊥inates most pictures taken in the Globe Lane area. The main feature to be seen here is The Shrubbery (better known as 'The dock'), an enclosed area of ground that had recently been purchased by the new borough for public use. In 1912 this area round was to be enclosed by a dwarf stone wall. The brick wall that runs the length of Globe Lane is part of the wall that rcled the landward side of the Ordnance Wharf. (Medway Council, Medway Archives & Local Studies Centre)

pur Battery and Parade, *c*. 1901. Part of the Fort Amherst complex, Spur Battery is situated in the south-east corner of the nd to the east of Prince William's Battery. At this time the fort, although still in military hands, was little used. However, g the First World War it was to play a useful role in the housing of troops en route to France. (Medway Council, Medway ves & Local Studies Centre)

Sign of the Olde Kynges Heade public house (93 High Street), October 1975. This sign seems to have first appeared in the High Street in 1897. As for the public house, formerly a hotel, this has an even longer history, dating back to 1635. Sadly, neither the public house nor its sign survived the twentieth century, the pub having ceased to trade in the 1990s. The former Olde Kynges Heade had become a professional ski shop by the end of the twentieth century. (Author)

Luton Arches viewed from the west, c. 1910. Situated at the east end of the High Street, this area of the town has always rather untidy feel, attracting as it does a mass of advertisements and hoardings. In this view, Spencer Pianos and Hovis are prominently advertised. The photographer has also caught a speeding train passing through to Gillingham while a trundles out of Luton Road. (Author)

The Chatham Memorial Fountain, *c.* 1901. At one time this was a very real landmark, but the fountain, together with its horse trough, has long since been removed for the purpose of aiding traffic flow. It was erected in 1899 as a memorial to Joshua Driver by his son, Cllr W.D. Driver. The latter represented the Luton ward on the borough council from 1896 to 1905 when he was elected an alderman. (Medway Council, Medway Archives & Local Studies Centre)

The Chapel, Royal Naval Barracks, *c.* 1920. Here, personnel posted to the Chatham naval barracks had to attend reg
Sunday service. (Author)

Waghorn Memorial in Maidstone Road, *c.* 1910. This is one of the few areas of Chatham that has undergone little change. Waghorn Memorial was first erected in 1888 and unveiled by the Earl of Northbrook. It commemorates the deeds of Lt erick Waghorn, a native of Chatham who pioneered the overland route to India. To the extreme left of this photo can just en the memorial to the crew of HMS *Barfleur*. During a posting to China between 1898 and 1902, twenty-one of her crew and their names are recorded on the obelisk. (Author)

ite, *bottom:* The Terrace, Chatham Royal Naval Barracks, *c.* 1910. Situated close to the dockyard, the barracks were ically outside the borough of Chatham. However, most of the servicemen posted there would frequently descend upon the s music halls, cinemas and theatres. For this reason, together with the official Chatham designation of the barracks, they been included in this book. For those in training, or awaiting transfer to a new ship, the accommodation provided by the cks was a marked improvement upon the old wooden hulks. (Author)

Dock Road, *c.* 1947. Stretching the full length of this photograph are the Royal Marine Barracks with the Guardroom Gate nearest to the camera. Much further to the right can be seen the main entry point to the barracks and beyond this are the officers' quarters. All these structures were added to the barracks during the late nineteenth century. Clearly this area of Chatham has changed considerably – a Royal Marine cycling into town being just one of the sights lost to the area. As for the barracks, these were officially closed in 1950. (*Kent Today*)

Kitchener Barracks, *c.* 1960. One of the few Chatham military buildings to survive the entire twentieth century, the barr
stand on Dock Road immediately opposite the site of the former Royal Marine Barracks. The first purpose-built mili
accommodation in the area, they were constructed between 1757 and 1760. The buildings in the photograph are of a n
later date. In the bottom left-hand corner it is just possible to see demolition work in progress at the old Marine barr
(Medway Council, Medway Archives & Local Studies Centre)

...ham's first public library (left) pictured in 1984, shortly before its demolition. It was necessary to remove this building ...ake way for the construction of a new footbridge that was to cross over a widened New Road. The library was first ...ed in 1903 and ceased to function when a central library was opened in Riverside Gardens. (Author)

ite, bottom: Bessent's Wharf, 1925. At one time a number of wharves existed along the small stretch of waterfront that ... behind the High Street and alongside Medway Street. Among the companies using this area at the time of the photograph ...Elders & Fyffes (banana importers) and W. Weddel & Co. (meat importers). As for C. Bessent & Son (who had their offices in ...rook), they were timber merchants, importing fir and other timbers from the Baltic. (Medway Council, Medway Archives ...al Studies Centre)

Sun Wharf Development Project, April 1983. This project necessitated the removal of several buildings in the section of the High Street where the Sun Hotel was once located. In the 1990s, the studios of BBC Radio Kent, together with the showrooms of Gransden Marine, moved into the area. (Author)

Altar of St Michael's Church, c. 1950. St Michael's is Chatham's Roman Catholic church and is located in Ordnance Erected between 1862 and 1863 at a cost of £3,000, it was built on a site purchased from the War Department. A sanctuary and side chapels were added in 1935, increasing the number of seats to 450. (Author)

The southern end of Globe Lane looking towards the High Street, June 1983. Now completely obliterated, having been demolished in the mid-1980s to make way for a raised section of road, it once connected the High Street and Medway Street. The decision to construct the overhead road also saw the removal of Dan's Alley, the roadway at the far end that runs further north. The large building partly visible at the junction is Lloyd's Bank (142 High Street), but only a part of this building still remains. (Author)

New Road, April 1987. This is a general view of an area that is constantly undergoing redevelopment. The three high blocks (Wellington, Regent and Steddy's Courts) were built during the mid-1960s and replaced the terraced housing of Pro Row. The overhead footbridge, a new landmark from which this photograph was taken, had only just been completed. (Au

The Dockyard main gate, c. 1910. Probably Chatham most famous landmark, thi gateway has served as the entrance to the dockyard si completion in 1720. (Auth

Cooper Row, Chatham Dockyard, September 1975. The one-time functional utility of the dockyard can be readily appreciated from this view of the Pattern Store. Built as a mast house, and now housing the Wooden Walls exhibition, it was at that time still covered in the fireproof cladding that had been fixed to it during the 1930s, a period when aerial bombardment of the yard was much feared. (Author)

Medway Street, March 1985. The terraced houses on the right, which were demolished in 1987, were once owned by the Edward Bates department store, this shop being close by in the High Street. At one time, these houses were occupied by staff employed in the alteration of clothing and made-to-measure wear. Nowadays, the area where these houses stood is the forecourt of a used car lot. (Author)

Railway Street, March 1984. In the last few years of the twentieth century, this area underwent further change particular, the town's ring road ran immediately behind St John's church. Dominating the skyline is Mountbatten H while St John's Church (constructed between 1819 and 1821) is seen on the left. (Author)

er Street Chapel, September 1986. One of the architectural gems of the town, this building was demolished in early 2001.
east dwellers of twentieth-century Chatham were able to benefit from this rather glorious building. This view shows the
e looking east. (Author)

Street Chapel, viewed from the upper balcony, September 1986. (Author)

Medway Arts Centre and Brook Theatre, September 1999. This fine building was officially opened as the Town Hall in 1900, and its balcony was once used to announce parliamentary and borough council election results. Huge crowds assembled for the purpose of cheering or jeering at the success of a Conservative, Labour or Liberal candidate. At different times throughout the twentieth century Chatham was represented in Parliament by all three parties. (Author)

Commercial Prosperity

Watts Place, looking towards the High Street, June 1931. At one time this tiny shop-lined street connected the High Street and Medway Street but it was all swept away upon the building of stores for both Edward Bates and Sainsbury's. The Sultan Inn was located on the east side opposite a café which changed hands regularly. Immediately next to Jeff's café was Ernest Lambert's hairdresser's shop. (*Kent Today*)

The central section of the High Street, *c.* 1901. Few of these shop buildings still exist in their original form. Those on the right (the north side) were removed to make way for the Pentagon while those opposite have seen many changes. A.J. Whitehead's (195–199 High Street) stood on this site for many years, trading as the complete house furnishers. On the south side note the sign to the Long Bar of the United Services public house. Popular with the Royal Marines, it was infamous for frequent fights and the consequent attendance of the Military Provost. (Author)

Luton Arches viewed from the east, *c.* 1905. The arches were at the furthest end of the High Street where it connects with New Road. The number of shops in the area has mu diminished. (Author)

A Delce-bound tram proceeds along Military Road, *c.* 1910. In the foreground are the premises of Richard Wade & Son, military outfitters. A number of similar shops were once situated in this area of Chatham. (Author)

Frederick Clark & Sons, motor bo and van builders, *c.* 1930. Situate the corner of New Road and Frede Street, the garage was subsequen renamed New Road Garage, but neither the garage nor the buildi still survives. Both Frederick Stre and the nearby Jeyes Street have ceased to exist. (Author)

The Royal Emporium (154–158 High Street), *c. 1920*. One of the largest stores on the High Street, the Royal Emporium was owned by George Church. It ceased trading in 1934 when the premises were acquired by Marks & Spencer. Adjoining it are the premises of Freeman, Hardy & Willis accommodated in the unusually named Elephant Buildings (152 High Street). (Medway Council, Medway Archives & Local Studies Centre)

Marks & Spencer Penny Bazaar, *c.* 1915. This was the first Marks & Spencer store in Chatham and was located east of Military Road at 167–169 High Street. (Marks & Spencer plc)

Marks & Spencer's new store, *c.* 1930. This photo was clearly taken after the move to the Royal Emporium premises, with shoppers encouraged to browse through a new range of spring and summer drapery. (Marks & Spencer plc)

e London
ircutting & Shaving
loon (375 High
eet), 16 April
30. Situated on
corner of Cage
ne (which no
ger exists) and the
gh Street, this was
e of a number of
ops which offered
le customers
h haircutting
d shaving services
le women could
into a private room
bobbing (short
geboy cut) and
ngling (a layered
). (Author)

Jay's Furnishing Stores
(78–80 High Street),
c. 1935. At this time
Jay's was a large
national company,
but had only recently
become established in
Chatham, having acquired
ownership of the Chatham
Furnishing Company.
The company remained at
these premises for several
decades. The adjoining
jeweller's shop of G.H.
de la Cour (76 High
Street) survived into the
1950s. (Medway Council,
Medway Archives & Local
Studies Centre)

43

The Chatham Motor Co., Railway Street, November 1937. Established in 1924 by Fred Mannington and Bill Tomlin, the company initially specialized in the sale of American-import Chevrolets. (Chatham Motor Company)

The brilliantly lit showroom of Chatham Motor Co., November 1937. The poster declares the company's connection with Vauxhall, it having acquired agency rights in 1932. (Chatham Motor Company)

PHONE 41222/5

The Chatham Motor Co Ltd

RAILWAY ST.
CHATHAM

VAUXHALL
SER**V**ICE
BEDFORD

MAIN DEALERS

A newspaper advertisement for the Chatham Motor Co., 1961. (Author)

atham Motor Co. vehicle
rk, *c.* 1960. Having
quired agency rights for
th Vauxhall and Bedford,
e company became a
ain supplier of these
akes to various statutory
encies including the
nt Ambulance Service.
hatham Motor Company)

ham Hill, 1913. The mist-enshrouded tram is on Route 3 to Rainham. The confectioner's shop, at one time owned by
am George Isles, was the last shop in Chatham before entering the borough of Gillingham. (Medway Council, Medway
ives & Local Studies Centre)

A busy High Street scene, *c.* 1929. Timothy White's chemist's shop (126 High Street) is to be seen on the left while tallest of the buildings on the right is Barnard's New Palace of Varieties (107–109 High Street). Timothy White's eventually amalgamated with Boots the Chemist. (Author)

Intersection of Military Road and High Street, *c.* 1930. A newly constructed building has just been taken over by Montague Burton Ltd, subsequently Burton's (139–143 High Street). The Red Lion public house (147 High Street) is located on opposite corner. (Author)

snow-covered Military Road, January 1962. This was a particularly bitter winter and the heavy snow briefly brought
atham to a standstill. Before the construction of the Pentagon, Military Road served as the town's bus terminal, with stops for
services lining this road. (*Kent Today*)

Hotel, *c.* 1929. W.H. Smith's had their original Chatham store in this part of the town (95–97 High Street) and the store is
ly seen on the left. The heavily laden lorry is coming out of Medway Street. It has probably collected its bags of flour from
own mill that then stood adjacent to Sun Pier. (Author)

A newspaper advertisement for 'the best drapers in Chatham', Edward Bates, 1926. Their premises at that time were those of Manor House, located in the High Street close to Manor Road. (Author)

Drawing of the planned new department store, c. 1960. The subsequent construction of this store, to be shared by Edward Bates and Sainsbury's, necessitated the demolition of Watts Place. The new store was completed in 1962. (Author)

ntall's High Street store, 1984. By this time
e 'new' department store built in 1962 had
en bought by Bentall's for £250,000. A further
00,000 was spent on refurbishment. Bentall's,
wever, could not maintain the store at a profit
d the building was subsequently aquired by Argos.
uthor)

w: The site of the former Sun Hotel, April 1983.
high-rise building on the right is Anchorage
se, which stands on the former site of the Chatham
ire. (Author)

Another changing area of the High Street, 1983
In later years this view would be impossible to reproduce as part of the scene was annihilated by the John Hawkins flyover that also helped ensure economic decline for businesses in this area. Fortunately, the flyover has now been demolished, with a return to prosperity hopefull on its way. Midway up on the right is Dan's Alley, which no longer exists. (Author)

The west end of Chatham High Street, 1985. Again, the changes here have been significant, not least the loss of the florists Lawrence (2 High Street). Their shop had stood on this site from at least 1918. (Author)

A Working Life

The Chatham seaman, *c.* 1915. At the beginning of the twentieth century naval seamen were a common sight in the streets of Chatham, the town having a large naval barracks at HMS *Pembroke*. (Author)

The petty officers' canteen, Chatham Naval Barracks, c. 1910. The naval barracks were first opened in April 1903, provi‹ Chatham-based seamen with relatively comfortable conditions. (Author)

The ratings' canteen, c. 1910. Most of the seamen posted to the naval barracks at Chatham appear to remember one above all else: this was the harsh discipline, bolstered by the senseless tasks frequently set to occupy them. (Author)

roup photo consisting primarily of petty officers permanently shore-based at Chatham, taken at Chatham Naval Barracks, *c.* 0. (Author)

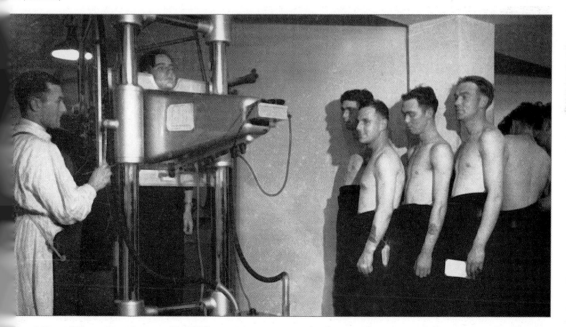

Royal Navy fights tuberculosis, *c.* 1945. This wartime propaganda photograph was intended to reassure families that who joined the navy were properly looked after. Here, the shore-based seamen of Chatham barracks undergo chest s. (Imperial War Museum, A2006)

The Luton hop pickers, *c.* 1920. Surprisingly, Chatham (or more precisely Luton village) was once a centre for hop-growing. Du
the month of September large numbers of female hop-pickers were to be seen on several farms in this area. Most of them were lo
recruited, and doubtless their husbands and sweethearts were employed in the dockyard. (Mr and Mrs Burrows)

Dockyard female labour, 1917. The contrast with the rustic charms of the female hop-picker could hardly have been gr
The wartime crisis, with hundreds of dockyard workers recruited into the services, led to a large number of women wo
entering the yard. To ensure that they were of immediate value, they did not undergo a lengthy apprenticeship, being tr
instead to undertake very specific tasks. (Chatham Dockyard Historical Society)

...ve: An early morning milk delivery in the dockyard, *c.* 1910. The
...man was Richard Sheepwash and his round took in the Reserve fleet
...d within the dockyard. His customers were the various ship-keepers
... oversaw the upkeep of these vessels, which were held at Chatham
...se in any sudden emergency. (Medway Council, Medway Archives &
...l Studies Centre)

...man William Paine, 1914. A man who dedicated much of his
... the needs of Chatham, he was a founder of Paine's outfitters
...erly of 168 High Street). In November 1900 he sought election
... council, successfully standing in St Mary's ward. His continuous
...bership of the council did not begin until 1909. In 1912 he
...ne an alderman before being elected mayor. In fact, he was one
...atham's longest-serving mayors, holding office for seven terms
...8–19). (Rochester Museum)

A visit to the hairdressers, *c.* 1910. Situated in Luton High Street, the Army & Navy Toilet Saloon was owned by James Turner. Always a busy shop, it offered a complete range of services that included shaving, singeing for a closer cut and the sale of various hair-care products including perfumes. (Author)

Below: The cruiser HMS *Arethusa* under construction, 5 April 1933. Arethusa was laid down on the no. 8 slip January 1933 and was launched on 6 March 1934. She was an important vessel for Chatham as she brought work at a time of high unemployment. (Chatham Dockyard Historical Society)

...atham High Street, 9 September 1939. ...e war had been declared six days earlier. ...r raids were expected and members of ...e County Constabulary had already ...en issued with metal helmets. This local ...obby' appears to have military assistance ...hand. At that time the town police ...tion was located in New Road Avenue. *...ent Today*)

...w: Luton Road First Aid Post, 1943. ...unteer workers in their wartime ...orms were constantly at the ready to ...l with any injuries caused by enemy ...ttack. (Medway Council, Medway ...hives & Local Studies Centre)

Fire drill, 1943. It seems likely that this photograph, depicting naval fire-fighters in training, was taken in the grounds of the naval barracks. (Imperial War Museum A17503)

Below: Mobile kitchen, 1943. As in the First World War, a huge number of additional workers were brought into the dockyard during the war years to help ensure a fast turn-around in ship repair work. Supporting these additional workers, mobile kitchens became an essential feature of the wartime dockyard. (Imperial War Museum A6443)

dockyard ropery, 1963. This part of the dockyard had seen the
loyment of women since 1865. Initially, those employed were
wives or widows of those seriously injured or killed in naval
ockyard service. By the 1960s this was no longer the case.
tham Dockyard Historical Society)

ntrance to the dockyard spinning room, 1990. When women
first employed in the ropery, numerous special rules kept them
ate from the men. At one time the women not only started
nished work at different times, but they also had a separate
ice. (Author)

The dockyard ropery, 1963. Women workers preparing fibres of manila hemp ready for transfer to the rope-laying floor. (Chatham Dockyard Historical Society)

Dockyard caulkers, 1963. Caulking is the process of filling the seams between the timbers to make the ship watertight. At one time, when all ships were built of timber, the dockyard employed over a hundred caulkers. However, the trade declined with the navy's conversion to iron ships, with the caulkers then being employed on ships' boats. The man on the right is using a hammer and caulking mallet. (Chatham Dockyard Historical Society)

ckyard no. 7 slip,
1970. This building played
rucial role in the history of
 yard, being used for the
 struction
 ubmarines. On
 September 1966
 atham's last submarine,
 anagan, was launched
 n the no. 7 slip, and the
 ding was subsequently
 d for storage. (Chatham
 kyard Historical Society)

o. 3 basin, c. 1984. Immediately prior to the closure of the dockyard, the no. 3 basin was taken over by the Medway Ports
rity as part of a new complex. Here, eight separate berths were created. (Chatham Dockyard Historical Society)

The Leander-class frigate HMS *Sirius* (F40), *c.* 1980. At the entrance to the Medway, Sirius is proceeding up-river to the dockyard at Chatham where she is due for a refit. In the years immediately before the closure of the dockyard, Chatham specializ[ed] in the refit of both Leander-class frigates and hunter-killer nuclea[r] submarines. (Author)

The Bull's Nose, *c.* 1976. This time the Leander-class frigate entering the dockyard is Diomede (F16). The Bull's Nose w[as] entry point to the dockyard basins and it was through here that a succession of ships entered the dockyard througho[ut] twentieth century. (Chatham Dockyard Historical Society)

Saints Hospital, 1985. The site was originally
uired in the nineteenth century as the Union
r House for Chatham and the surrounding
shes. One of the duties of the original poor
commissioners was that of health care, and
his reason a small nursing ward was added to
workhouse. It was out of this that All Saints
oital was created. Even as late as the 1980s,
rly members of the Chatham community found
ficult to enter the hospital, remembering its
er harsher days – when the likelihood was that
would never leave the building again, other
i in a wooden box. (Author)

edlewomen of All Saints Hospital, 1950. Second from the left is Ethel Tester, née Croucher, who lived at 34 The Brook.
ork of the needlewomen was mainly confined to the repair of hospital linen and surgical clothing. (Clive Tester)

The river trade, October 1982. These tugs belonging to J.P. Knight were once a regular sight around Chatham frequently engaged in guiding vessels into the local ports. The J.P Knight fleet was sold in 1991. (Author)

A return to the old days, June 1990. The no. 4 dry dock at Chatham dockyard, which was originally built to accommodate the old 'wooden walls', sees the welcome return of a sailing ship. (Author)

To Entertain

Reviewed as a 'weak melodrama', Mr Wu was showing at the National Electric Theatre in March 1929. Situated in the central section of the High Street, the National Electric was Chatham's first purpose-built cinema and was opened in December 1911. (Author)

Above: Barnard's New Palace of Varieties, *c.* 1905. First opened in 1885, this was an outstandingly successful music hall that was popular with the m[...] soldiers stationed at Chatham. It was demolished [...] 1934 following a disastrous fire that had broken [...] in March of that year. (Author)

The site of the former Barnard's New Palace of Varieties, October 1984. This photograph was ta[...] from a similar position to the one above, showing[...] edge of No. 105, then a florist's. In the top pictur[...] these same premises were owned by Rego Clothi[...] Ltd, tailors. (Author)

e Theatre Royal, March 1999. Originally opened in July
99, the Theatre Royal was designed to bring touring
atre companies to Chatham and it offered a contrast to
vibrant music halls that existed in this area of the High
et. Efforts made to restore this historic building to its
ginal design and purpose failed, although the structure
y find a future alternative use. (Author)

Memorial to Daniel Barnard, October 1980. Daniel Barnard
was the senior member of the Barnard family and was largely
responsible for bringing the music hall to Chatham. His sons
went on to establish both the New Palace of Varieties and
the Theatre Royal. Daniel Barnard died on 26 October 1879
and his tomb is to be found in the graveyard of the Chatham
synagogue. (Author)

The Empire Theatre, *c.* 1955. The Empire, which first opened in March 1912, was a variety theatre designed to compete with Barnard's. During the First World War a cinema called the Picture Palace was added to the complex. The entrance to the cinema, which by the time of this photograph had been renamed the Empire, can be seen to the left of the canopied entrance to the theatre. (*Kent Today*)

Chatham Hill, *c.* 1920. Clearly visible to tram passengers and pedestrians passing between Chatham and Gillingham was this huge billboard advertisement for the Empire. Along the wall below are various fly postings, some of them advertising forthcoming cinema and variety events. (Medway Council, Medway Archives & Local Studies Centre)

Gaiety Theatre, June 1906. Topping the bill on this occasion was Florrie Forde, the Australian chorus singer whose most famous number was 'Down at the Old Bull and Bush'. The Gaiety Theatre was later transformed into the Empire Theatre. (Author)

The National Electric Theatre, *c.* 1920. Established in 1911, the National Electric Theatre continued showing films u
February 1950. Subsequently it became a clothes shop. This building is still to be found in the High Street, close to
Pentagon shopping centre. (Brian Joyce)

How films used to be advertised, February 1932. In the background is Chatham station while St John's Church can also be
in the background. The film was showing at the Picture House (formerly the Imperial Picture Palace) and concerned a y
boy's faith in a 'washed-up' boxer – so explaining the set-piece cameo. (*Kent Today*)

: Arthur Allen, former manager of the ABC
nema, June 1983. Mr Allen (left) had a
nsiderable interest in the history of Medway
nemas and established a small museum at the
BC. Among the exhibits were model cinema
gans similar to those that once existed in the
o Chatham super-cinemas: the Regent (later
ABC and Canon) and the Ritz. Mr Allen is
en here with fellow cinema enthusiast Mr
mp. (Mr A. Allen)

The entrance to the Invicta Cinema,
c. 1930. The Invicta, one of three
cinemas in the Medway Towns owned
by the Croneen family, was situated at
the end of Fullager's Alley, immediately
next to Woolworth's. It was originally
opened in 1916. (Clive Tester)

changing styles of the cinema
rette, Chatham Super Regent,
3. This picture forms an interesting
cast with that of the National
ric staff of the 1920s (see p. 70
Left to right: Molly Sinclair, Joan
ell, Betty L'Amie, Irene Munn
ma secretary), Gladys Farley, Vera
aine and Dorothy Pratt (sales girl).
A. Allen)

71

The demolition of the Invicta in Fullager's Yard, 20 March 1987. All that remained by that date was the circle and front façade. Although it began life in 1916 as a cinema, the Invicta later became a forces canteen, a ballroom and a venue for some of the most famous pop groups of the 1960s. (Author)

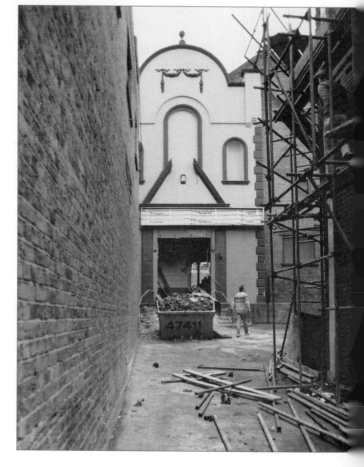

The front façade of the Invicta, 20 March 1987. Among the celebrities who trod the boards of the Invicta were the Beatles, the Rolling Stones and Jerry Lee Lewis. Less well known at the time was Wendy Richard, later of EastEnders fame, who also came to the Invicta, joining Mike Sarne in the singing of 'Come Outside'. A few weeks after this photograph was taken the building no longer existed, and Fullager's Alley was an anonymous entity. The site of the cinema is just another car park. (Author)

e Regent cinema,
April 1930. At the time it
as the largest of the Chatham
nemas and stood at the west
d of the High Street. In
'37 it was replaced by a new
ilding, the Super Regent,
ich subsequently became the
3C. (Medway Council, Medway
chives & Local Studies Centre)

Chatham ABC cinema, April
1984. Located on the site
of the first Regent cinema,
this was the Super Regent
built in 1937. By 1984
further conversions had
resulted in three separate
screens. The arrival of out-
of-town multiplex cinemas
resulted in the closure of
this building as a cinema
and eventual replacement.
(Author)

73

Building of the Ritz cinema, October 1935. The Ritz, which also stood at the west end of the High Street, was eventually ope
by Jack Buchanan in March 1937. A massive Wurlitzer organ provided an additional attraction to various films sho
(Author)

The Ritz, April 1984. Having started life as a super-cinema, the Ritz spent its final days as a bingo and social club. (Author)

at the former Ritz cinema, September 1998. Following this disastrous fire, the building was completely demolished and aced by a purpose-built bingo hall. (*Kent Today*)

g the foundation stone of the Wesleyan mission, later Central Hall, 18 April 1907. It was much praised for the quality of oductions, with regular visits by various national and international stars. (Author)

Chatham Cycling Club, *c.* 1901. Not all of Chatham's leisure activities were based around the cinema and theatre. H members of the local cycling club pose for a photograph before a ride out into the countryside. (Medway Council, Med\ Archives & Local Studies Centre)

The Welcome Sailors & Soldiers Home, *c.* 1930. Designed as a counter-attraction to the red ligh area of The Brook, the Welcome provided alco free entertainment and overnight accommodat for Chatham-based sold and sailors. (Author)

Hen and Chickens, Luton, 1909. This was one of the numerous public houses that existed throughout the borough [C]hatham. Unlike those in the High Street, the Hen and Chickens was rarely frequented by the military. In fact, given its [pro]ximity to the Luton tram depot, many of its customers were probably employed by the 'Chatham & District' as either tram [crew] or maintenance workers. (Author)

[...] billiards room, [C]ham Naval [Barr]acks, c. 1910. [Ra]nge of entertainment [...] offered within the [nava]l barracks, although [ratin]gs much preferred [to ge]t away from the [restr]ictions of barrack [...] [f]acilities included [readi]ng rooms, a [swi]mming pool, a library [and t]his finely laid out [billia]rds room. (Author)

The bowling hall of the Chatham Na[...]
Barracks, *c.* 1910. (Author)

The *Evening Post* offices, April 1984[...]
evening daily newspaper, the *Evenin[...]
Post was first published on
6 August 1968. In its first year it
had a temporary rival in the form o[...]
the *Evening Mail*, a newspaper that
survived a mere seven weeks. In tu[...]
the *Evening Post* became *Kent Today[...]
a newspaper that provided a numb[...]
of the photographs in this book.
In turn, *Kent Today* (subsequently
Medway Today) closed in April 200[...]
replaced by the twice weekly *Medw[...]
Messenger. (Author)

Media House, October 1990. This building, which stands at the foot of Gundulph Road, has a long connection with the mass media. In its early days it was used by Parrett & Neves, proprietors of the Chatham News (now Medway News). Later it became the studios of Radio Medway, before its transition into Radio Kent. Since then, Radio Kent has moved to nearby Sun Pier. (Author)

Radio Caroline off Sun Pier, 25 January 1996. An unexpected visitor to Chatham was the Ross Revenge, the ship that operated in the North Sea as Radio Caroline. Plans at that time existed for Radio Caroline to broadcast from Chatham, but nothing came of this idea. (Author)

A lavish production at the Royal Naval Barracks, September 1913. In that year the seamen of HMS *Pembroke* upstaged cinemas and music halls of the town when they re-enacted scenes from the Boxer Uprising. (Author)

The cast of the spectacular Boxer Uprising pageant pose for the camera, September 1913. Over a period of several days pe living in Chatham were invited to visit the barracks so that they might see at first hand the opportunities available throu naval career. The re-creation of the Boxer Uprising, which served as the daily finale, included a typical Chinese street scene a realistic mock battle. (Author)

he Regent, *c.* 1950. As well as showing
ms, the Regent also offered live music.
ere, the Reg Simpson Band is playing to a
cked audience. The screen of the cinema,
ith its curtained front, provides a back-
op. (Brian Joyce)

Modern entertainment versus the theatre,
June 1986. To the left is a specialized video
shop while diagonally opposite is the old
Theatre Royal building. The theatre failed
to survive the vicissitudes of passing time
and by this time housed a sports shop.
(Author)

Bingo, November 2000. It was the Ritz,
is very site, that had first introduced the
g of bingo. After the building's destruction
e, it was replaced by the purpose-built Gala
Club. (Author)

Navy Days, May 1978. Proving that the navy could still upstage all other local entertainers, Navy Days was undoubtedly the most popular show ever produced in Chatham. Each year it attracted thousands upon thousands, with the last Navy Days held in 1981. (Author)

Rolls-Royce rally, June 1990. The Historic Dockyard, which first began attracting visitors in the mid-1980s, organizes a number of outstanding events. In 1990 it was decided to celebrate the Rolls-Royce, with owners bringing their much-admired machines to the dockyard for the day. (Author)

Be it Ever so Humble

Gibraltar Place, New Road, 1994. These houses were built in 1794, so this was the year of their bicentenary. Over those two hundred years they had provided Chatham with an attractive terrace and in earlier years accommodation there had been much sought after by army and navy officers, together with senior dockyard personnel. (Author)

Cross Street, *c*. 1910. These houses, since demolished, had seen much better days. Originally built in the seventeenth century to provide accommodation for dockyard officers, their age and frequent sub-tenanting had resulted in the houses having become considerably less desirable. (Author)

...ll-a-Love Alley, *c.* 1901. This photograph ...s taken when Full-a-Love Alley was on the ...rge of demolition. For many years this street ...d been condemned by the health authority, ...old poorly drained houses proving a health ...zard for all those who lived there. After the ...noval of the houses, the alley was replaced ...the wider Bachelor Street. (Medway Council, ...dway Archives & Local Studies Centre)

...w: Capstone Farmhouse, *c.* 1901. By ...trast with the tightly packed housing of ...ral Chatham there is the idyllic charm of ...still surviving building. Capstone Farm was ...of the farms in the Luton area that once ...ided Chatham's market with much-needed ...produce. (Author)

Queen Street, south side, c. 1930. At that time, it was one of the poorest areas of Chatham, and there was widespread concern about the well-being of those who lived there. Shortly after this photograph was taken, much of Queen Street was demolished and its inhabitants rehoused. Subsequently, council houses were built in this street, together with nearby King Street and Cross Street. (Fine Arts Studio)

Cross Street, *c.* 1930. This is another view of the impoverished area of Chatham, taken shortly before the people of this st were removed and their houses demolished. (Fine Arts Studio)

Washing day, Cross Street, *c.* 1930. The markings on the door indicate that this is the back of no. sixteen. At that time Mrs lived here, but it is not recorded if these were all her children. She was rehoused in one of the newly built houses in Syr Avenue after the demolition of Cross Street. (Fine Arts Studio)

st Street, *c.* 1920. Long-since
nolished, these seventeenth-
ntury houses were another
ght on the town of Chatham.
wadays, of course, Best Street
ks any housing, being part of
town's ring road. It is lined
car parks and various faceless
dings. (Author)

village, *c.* 1920. The introduction of the tram and the expansion of the dockyard brought considerable changes to the
ural aspect of Luton, the village becoming rapidly urbanized from about 1885 onwards. Many of the houses seen in this
would have been occupied by people employed in the dockyard. (Les Collins)

The Davis Estate, Chatham, 15 August 1940. Much of the housing on the Davis Estate was constructed during the 1930s offered a modern style of house in sharp contrast to the densely packed terraced houses of the town centre. Unfortunately houses in this particular area suffered considerable damage as a result of German bombing. The target was nearby Roche airport where Short Stirlings were under construction. (*Kent Today*)

Ordnance Street, 6 October 1940. Chatham was very much on the front line during the Battle of Britain, and rarely a day by when the sirens did not sound or air raids take place. The target was invariably the dockyard – and its workforce. I the afternoon of 5 October bombs fell across Ordnance Place causing severe damage both to these houses and to John Mission. (*Kent Today*)

...ant Street, 1961.
...ese Victorian terraces
...re originally built
...accommodate the
...rkforce of the rapidly
...anding dockyard.
...s photograph was
...en shortly before
...ch of this area was
...olished. (Medway
...ncil, Medway
...hives & Local Studies
...tre)

The east side of
Claremont Place,
1961. Again,
considerable
changes have been
made to this area of
Chatham, with an
underpass allowing
easy access from
the town. (Medway
Council, Medway
Archives & Local
Studies Centre)

A Chatham family, *c.* 1936. Ethel Tester née Croucher (centre right) with her twin sister Dolly (left) and two young children, Daphne (right) and Vic. The photograph was probably taken in the back garden of 14 Garden Row where Ethel lived with her husband Albert. At that time Albert was employed in the dockyard ropery, having served on board the cruiser Boadicea during the First World War. Garden Row, one of the many roads removed to make way for the construction of the Pentagon, was within easy walking distance of the dockyard, although Albert would have found it easier to catch one of the frequent buses that then operated from near Military Road. (Clive Tester)

The Croucher family, photographed in the backyard of their house at 34 The Brook, *c.* 1953. The Brook was another of the densely packed streets removed for the building of the Pentagon. George Croucher (back row, right) was employed in the dockyard, as was his brother Eric. Included in the photograph are George's sister Dolly and his mother Emily. (Clive Tester)

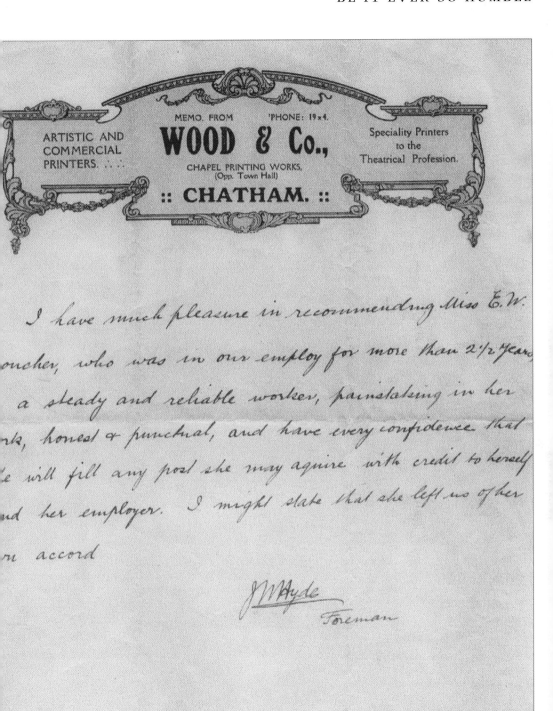

ARTISTIC AND
COMMERCIAL
PRINTERS.

MEMO. FROM   'PHONE: 19x4.

WOOD & Co.,

CHAPEL PRINTING WORKS,
(Opp. Town Hall)

:: CHATHAM. ::

Speciality Printers
to the
Theatrical Profession.

I have much pleasure in recommending Miss E. W. Croucher, who was in our employ for more than 2½ years, a steady and reliable worker, painstaking in her work, honest & punctual, and have every confidence that she will fill any post she may aquire with credit to herself and her employer. I might state that she left us of her own accord

JW Hyde
Foreman

...from Wood & Co., *c.* 1920. The letter gives a reference for Ethel Croucher (see previous page) and refers to her work ...he firm of printers. Located in The Brook for much of the early part of the twentieth century, they produced many of the ...ammes and advertisements used by Barnards, the Theatre Royal and the Empire. The site was located close to the present-...entagon shopping centre taxi pick-up point. (Clive Tester)

The west side of the Pentagon, October 2000. The construction of the Pentagon necessitated the destruction of much o
housing south of The Brook, including the houses where members of the Tester and Croucher families once lived. A photog
taken from the same place forty years earlier would have shown George Street (which ran east from Military Road) a
intersection with Nelson Road (which ran from The Brook). (Author)

PUBLIC HEALTH DEPARTMENT, CHATHAM.

Tree Lane, 1928. A very different form of home existed alongside Ash Tree Lane and close to Upper Luton. For many years was the site of a permanent travellers' encampment. As may be seen by the typed heading added to the photograph, the mpment was a subject of concern to the borough's public health department. (Medway Council, Medway Archives & Local es Centre)

ree Lane, 1955. Although this photograph was taken nearly forty years later, the encampment was little changed. ver, its location on top of Sugar Loaf Hill was about to be brought to an end, the site being denied to its homesteaders y after this photograph was taken. (Medway Council, Medway Archives & Local Studies Centre)

Command House, *c.* 1960. Situated within the area of th abandoned Ordnance Wharf, this was once the residence o the senior officer. Built durin; the eighteenth century, it car close to demolition after the closure of the Ordnance Wha Subsequently it became the Command House, a pleasant pub and restaurant situated the banks of the River Medw: (Medway Council, Medway Archives & Local Studies Cen

A general view of Chatham's central shopping and residential area, March 1996. Despite widespread demolition of of central Chatham – some of it worth demolishing, some not – the centre of the town has a very untidy appearance. distance a mass of housing spreads along the hill, while the three tower blocks (Steddy's, Wellington and Regent Cour located in an area once occupied by Prospect Row and Bryant Street. (Author)

A Moment in Time

Evacuation from Chatham, 1 September 1939. With the town and
dockyard a likely target for aerial bombardment, over two thousand
children were evacuated to the Kentish countryside. With the
subsequent fall of France and the possibility of invasion, many of these
children were once again moved. This time they were taken to the
safety of Wales, most of them remaining there until the latter part of
1944. (Imperial War Museum, HU 59253)

A military parade along Luton Road, c. 1910. Such parades were a regular feature of life in Chatham, the town possessing an navy and Royal Marine barracks. (Les Collins)

The Chatham field gun display team, September 1910. Held at the naval barracks, the competition was used to select men of the naval team that would eventually represent Chatham at the Royal Tournament. In essence, the competition simulat transfer of a field gun across a chasm and the rebuilding of the gun for action. The wooden wheels of the gun were maint and rebuilt by dockyard wheelwrights. (Author)

e Paddock, *c.* 1910.
:ated in the centre of
atham, the Paddock
:e offered a quiet
pite from the hectic
 n centre. It has since
 n replaced by a new
d system. (Author)

on parade in front of Chatham Town Hall, 20 April 1913. The Scouts are drawn up in preparation for the annual
rge's Day parade that will take them to the nearby parish church of St Mary's. Overseeing the event is the district
 naster, Mr A.J. Tassell. (Author)

Above: The Women's Auxiliary Army Corps Peace Day Parade 19 July 1919. To commemora the end of the First World War most towns in the country organized large-scale military processions. The one in Chath included all branches of the military, together with others had served during those despe times. So extended in length w the Chatham parade that it to twenty minutes to pass a give point. (Author)

HMS *Sterlet* in the River Med following her commissioning ceremony, 1938. Sterlet was of fifty-seven submarines buil Chatham, and she undertook service with the 3rd (Harwic Flotilla. Sadly, she was sunk the Skaggerak on 16 April 1 (Imperial War Museum, FL3

...cuation from Chatham, 1 September 1939. Two
...happy youngsters take leave of their parents on the
... of war. With hostilities declared just two days later,
...se children were probably not to return for almost five
...rs. Only teachers and others with very young children
...e allowed to accompany the evacuees. (Imperial War
...seum, HU59252)

...am Reach, August 1940. A lieutenant in the Royal Navy Volunteer Reserve ('the Wavy Navy') inspects the remains of a
...d Spitfire. (Imperial War Museum, A704)

Target Chatham, 1938. An aerial view of Chatham dockyard and the
surrounding area, as photographed by a German aeroplane prior to
the outbreak of war. The dockyard is spread out along the length of the
Medway, with the three large basins (a), used for the fitting and repair of
ships, clearly visible in the upper part of the photograph. Also to be seen
are the various covered slips (f), dry docks (b) and ropery (k). Strangely,
the naval barracks (centre) are not marked as a target. (Imperial War
Museum, C5647)

War Weapons Week, 11 February 1941. With the war at its height the people of Chatham gather along The Brook to wi[...] a morale-raising military parade. The object was to draw attention to the borough's declared intention of raising £450,00[...] the building of a new destroyer. It was a target easily achieved. In this view of wartime Chatham it is clear that the Town [...] which started the war protected only by sandbags, has gained an anti-blast wall. Further along The Brook, where the Pent[...] now stands, can be seen Bernards Corner (the tailoring shop of C.H. Bernard) and the Salvation Army Naval & Military H[...] (*Kent Today*)

Main Gate, Royal Marine Barracks, Dock Road, 16 April 1942. King George VI makes a visit to the barracks. Th[...] newspaper photographer just caught the royal limousine as it disappeared inside the gate. (*Medway Today*)

tain trains her allies, May 1944.
the Chatham Naval Barracks a
up of lieutenants of the Imperial
nese Navy are undergoing training
he hands of a petty officer. During
wartime years Chatham developed
irly cosmopolitan feel, as a large
ber of foreign navies were making
of the dockyard and the training
ities at HMS *Pembroke*. (Imperial
r Museum, A30224)

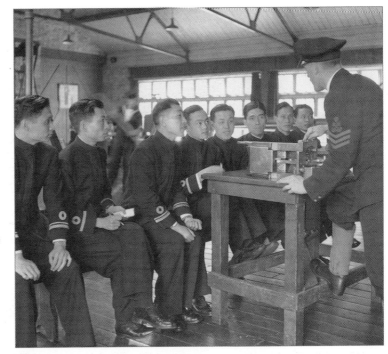

w: VE-Day commemorated, May
4. Don't be fooled by the appearance
is apparent wartime photograph.
uthentic as it may appear, it was
n in the dockyard at Chatham on
occasion of the fiftieth anniversary
E-Day. On that day the dockyard
taken over by the City of Rochester-
n-Medway for the purpose of
rating the event. (Author)

Dock Road at the intersection with Globe Lane 22 February 1946. It is the end of the working day and cyclists are on their way home from the dockyard. The buildings to the left belong to the Ordnance Wharf. (*Medway Today*)

Below: The hand-over of HMS *Achilles* to the Indian Navy, 5 July 1948. To mark this important occasion, an inspection parade was arranged at the naval barracks prior to the commissioning of HMS *Achilles* into the Royal Indian Navy as INS Delhi. (Imperial War Museum, HU35905)

Chatham Empire,
December 1944. With the
finally coming to an end, the
nts of Chatham began to
rward to a Christmas less
an the previous five. At
tham Empire, Steffani and
r Songsters performed a
of popular songs together
nge of carols. (Author)

The hockey team, HMS *Pembroke*,
May 1952. Following a successful
season, the members of the team
sit back to savour the moment.
(Author)

e nice girls love a sailor –
ham dockyard, *c.* 1967. Following
onclusion to a successful Navy
, a young naval cadet poses for
oto with two young admirers.
hor)

The devastated hide-out of Alan Derek Poole, Symo[ns] Avenue, 6 June 1951. Following a massive po[lice] operation to arrest Po[ole] the murderer of Police Constable Alan Baxte[r], [he] was eventually found [at his] parents' home in Sy[mons] Avenue. Refusing to [be] taken alive, Poole c[hose to fire] with a sten gun. Th[e police] returned fire, a ma[ssive] fusillade leading in[evitably to] Poole's death. (Ken[t] Constabulary)

HMS *Blake* enters Chatham dockyard, January 1980. Having been converted to a helicopter cruiser, the large wa[rship] proved extremely expensive to maintain. For this reason she was directed to Chatham for laying-up prior to eventual dis[posal]. She was one of the largest ships held in the dockyard during the final years of its existence. (Author)

Endurance returns to Chatham, summer 1982. The Antarctic survey ship, having played a crucial role in that year's
[Falkla]nds campaign, is gently pushed to the quayside of the dockyard's no. 3 basin. Along the length of the lower Medway
[t]housands had turned out to watch her return, while a naval helicopter escort was also on hand. (Author)

[T]all Ships come to Chatham, July 1985. An important coup
[for th]e administrators of the former dockyard was that of arranging
[for th]e annual Tall Ships Race to be partly based at Chatham. The
[event] was well attended, with many thousands of visitors boarding
[the nu]merous sailing ships that arrived in Chatham throughout
[the m]onth. (Author)

The Festival of Culture, 5 September 1988. This used to be an annual North Kent festivity, and in 1988 it was the t
Chatham to act as host. Here, the organizers, together with the mayors and mayoresses of Rochester-Upon-Medway (
then included Chatham), Gravesend and Dartford pose for the camera. The event was a colourful spectacle that con
portrayed Chatham as a multi-cultural community. Another view of this important event can be found on page 10. (Auth

Celebrating the Chinese New Year in Chatham, February 2000. To celebrate the arrival of the Chinese new year, memb
the local community staged their famous dragon dance at the east end of the High Street. (*Kent Today*)

The Heritage
Industry

The historic figureheads outside the dockyard sailing centre,
September 1979. Since the closure of the dockyard, most of
the ships' figureheads that once abounded throughout the
yard have been removed. In the case of Britomart, the figure
nearest the sailing centre, it now stands within the Historic
Dockyard museum. The sailing centre itself, which was
originally built to accommodate the naval harbourmaster,
has also witnessed considerable change, and later served as a
restaurant. (Author)

Chatham dockyard museum, 1902. The original dockyard museum, established in about 1895, made the first real attempt preserve Chatham's heritage. The building, which no longer exists, appears on several dockyard maps between the nos 2 3 docks. Collective memory says that it was a specially built, prefabricated metal structure with extra large windows for provision of ample light. (Author)

The figurehead of the old wooden battleship HMS *Adelaide, c.* 1906. Once located within the grounds of the naval barracks, it was erected at the entrance to the new barracks following the selling of the ship out of naval service in 1905. (Author)

...dicea visits the Royal Marine Barracks, August 1912. This early example of historical re-enactment took place during the ...ual pageant of the Royal Marines. The theme of the 1912 pageant was a history of the British armed forces from the time of ...Romans, with one hapless 'volunteer' dressed as Queen Boadicea. (Author)

Royal Marine Barracks, August 1912. In all, 197 officers and men were involved in the depiction of the armed services in earlier centuries, with this group representing Roundheads and Cavaliers. (Author)

Above: No. 18 St Mary's Place, The Brook, 1943. The house under demolition was once the boyhood home of the novelist Charles Dickens. Admittedly, it was not his favourite residence, the family moving there during times of extreme hardship. Nevertheless, it seems an appalling loss to the town's heritage, as much could have been made of Chatham's connection with the author. Immediately next to the partially demolished house is the Ebenezer Congregational Chapel building (see opposite). (Medway Council, Medway Archives & Local Studies Centre)

No. 11 Ordnance Terrace, 1920. It was here, in 1817, that the Dickens family first lived on their arrival in Chatham. Despite the literary connections of this building, its state and condition throughout much of the twentieth century left much to be desired. Happily, in recent years, it has fallen into more caring hands. (Medway Council, Medway Archives & Local Studies Centre)

...ove: The Ebenezer Congregational Chapel in The Brook,
...il 1984. Constructed in 1858 on the site of an earlier
...pel, this building, now demolished, ended its life as a
...age. (Author)

Navy Week, Chatham, 1931. A scaled-down replica of an
eighteenth-century warship built by ratings from the naval
barracks. The vessel is HMS *Kent* and it is here seen in one of
the dockyard basins. (Author)

Lloyd's of London, June 1995. Situated alongside Dock Road, the grounds then occupied by Lloyd's once had strong naval connections. The area closest to Dock Road was formerly occupied by the Royal Marine Barracks, while that nearest to the river was the Ordnance Wharf. To mark the connection, a number of eighteenth-century guns mounted on naval carriages provide an ornate addition to the grass banks that overlook the Medway. (Author)

The Command House, June 1995. This interesting riverside pub, much frequented during summer months, was formerly the house of the commanding officer of the Ordnance Wharf. Here, in earlier times, warships entering the naval dockyard would have their ordnance maintained and repaired ready for their return to sea. (Author)

A wartime fast patrol craft passes the Lloyd's building, May 1995. This was one of the many vessels brought to Chatham for the purpose of celebrating the fiftieth anniversary of VE-Day. (Author)

The dockyard sawmill, September 2000. This unique building has yet to receive full recognition. Designed by Marc Brunel, sawmill utilized steam power both for the cutting of the timber and for its subsequent removal (via an overhead rail system the nearby timber pound. (Author)

The Dockyard Chapel, May 1986. For many years following the dockyard's closure many buildings had a 'Mary Celeste' feel. The abandoned chapel was no exception, although nowadays it has been returned to use as a conference centre. (Author)

dockyard no. 1 Smithy, March 1998. This was another of the buildings abandoned at the time of the yard's closure. At one the Historic Dockyard Trust hoped to make this building the centre-piece of a new heritage project that would focus on iron ship construction. Limited funds led to the abandonment of this particular project. (Author)

The smithy in March 1998 contained a veritable treasure-trove of industrial archaeology. The building was originally constructed in 1808 to a design by Edward Holl. For many years, due to the failure to aquire finance for the iron warship construction project, the building was at serious risk. Eventually, through support given by the Imperial War Museum and National Maritime Museum, the No. 1 Smithery is due to open in July 2010 as a cultural and learning activity centre. (Author)

The Mast House Mould Loft, *c.* 1970. Two members of the dockyard construction department consider the various ships whose lines were laid down on the mould loft floor. Before building a warship, it was normal to draw her lines out to scale, with templates subsequently cut. The first ship listed on this board, Achilles, was laid down on 1 August 1861. However, earlier ships were known to have had their lines drawn on this floor, these possibly including Victory, Nelson's flagship at Trafalgar. (Author)

submarine Ocelot entering dry dock, July 1992. An important occasion for the Historic Dockyard was the return of Ocelot ...e dockyard following her retirement from the navy. Originally launched at Chatham in May 1962, the submarine is now ...ermanent display in the yard. (Author)

HMS *Cavalier*, September 1999. A wartime destroyer, Cavalier is a recent addition to the dockyard. Her presence, together with Ocelot, has allowed the Historic Dockyard to attract larger numbers of visitors. (Author)

The battered Medway Queen lying off the dockyard, Decemb[...]
1984. The fear that this famous Medway vessel might be
permanently lost led to the formation of a small company
which was responsible for returning the ship to the Medwa[...]
Lack of money meant the vessel lay temporarily neglected [...]
before it was moved to Damhead Creek for restoration wo[...]
During the early part of 2010 the Medway Queen's hull
was being rebuilt in Bristol prior to being towed back to t[...]
Medway. (Author)

Below: Medway House, July 1978. One of the oldest houses i[...]
Chatham, Medway House was originally built for the dockya[...]
commissioner in 1703. The figureheads have since been
removed, with a number being located in the Museum of the
Royal Dockyard. (Author)

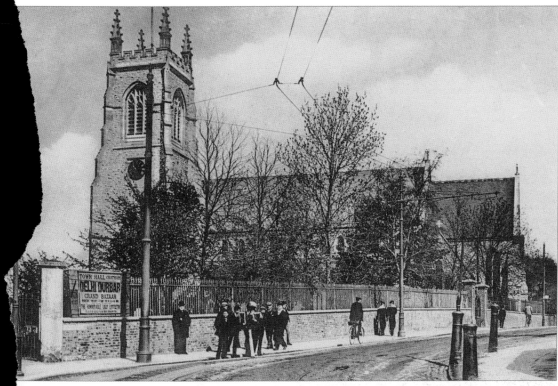

...ary's, the former parish church, March 1904. By the end of the twentieth century this magnificent building had ceased ...rseeing the spiritual needs of local parishioners. By 1984 it had been reopened as the Medway Heritage Centre, but in ...0 was unoccupied. (Author)

The defence of Fort Amherst, September 1986. French troops from the age of Napoleon lay siege to the fort, with British guns providing a thunderous response. Over the years Fort Amherst has become an extremely popular attraction. (Author)

123

HMS *Gannet* in Chatha[m] dockyard, June 1991. [...] Gannet, a nineteenth-century naval sloop, was built in the form[er] dockyard at Sheern[ess]. She was brought to Chatham in 1987 a[nd] since undergone e[xtensive] restoration that ha[s] turned her into a [major] visitor attraction. [...]

HMS *Gannet*, Chatham dockyard, 1993. Progress on the sloop was painfully slow, with only limited changes discernible. (Author)

HMS *Gannet*, Chatham dockyard, 2000. Progress is limited, though the vessel has been moved to a new dock, principally to make way for the arrival of Ocelot, the new dockyard showpiece. (Author)

Acknowledgements

In putting together this photographic history of Chatham, I am extremely grateful to a number of friends who were kind enough to allow me use of several personal photographs. I welcome the opportunity of acknowledging help given by Les Collins, ian Joyce and Clive Tester. I would also like to thank Arthur Allen, Peter Dawson and r and Mrs Burrows. In addition, I must record my gratitude to the following institutions that so permitted use of photographs: the Chatham Dockyard Historical Society, the Imperial ar Museum, the Kent Messenger Newspaper Group and Rochester Museum. I must also mention the Medway Archives and Local Studies Centre, with special acknowledgement to the members of staff, especially Norma Crowe for her patience and assistance.

Philip MacDougall
July 2002

Philip MacDougall has been researching and writing on the history of Chatham and the Medway area for over thirty years. His particular interest is the dockyard and he has written an impressive number of books on this subject alone. Among them is his most recent, a detailed study of Chatham dockyard during the early nineteenth century – a period in which it was undergoing a massive transformation as it adapted to new technologies. Philip was the first to develop the idea of Chatham as a unique industrial-military complex and which is paramount to the town's bid for World Heritage status. Having taught at the University of Kent, where he also gained his doctorate in history, Philip's attention is now concentrated upon further historical research and the publishing of his findings. Not surprisingly, there are a number of other Medway-connected books in the pipeline. For more information on the author, visit www.philipmacdougallbooks. co.uk.